BECOME A COSMETOLOGIST

Hairstyling, Skin Care & More

Margo Gates

Abdo & Daughters
MIDDLE GRADE NONFICTION
An imprint of Abdo Publishing
abdobooks.com

ABDOBOOKS.COM

Published by Abdo Publishing, a division of ABDO, PO Box 398166, Minneapolis, Minnesota 55439.

Printed in the United States of America, North Mankato, Minnesota
102024
012025

Design: Denise Hamernik, Mighty Media, Inc.
Production: Mighty Media, Inc.
Editor: Katherine Chu

Cover Photographs: Adobe Stock (hairdryer, lip gloss, nail polish, hair brush, hair trimmer, lipstick smudge); Shutterstock Images (blush powder, essential oils, eyeshadow, foundation, hair scissors, lipstick, makeup brushes, salon background)

Interior Photographs: Addison N. Scurlock/Wikimedia Commons, p. 6 (bottom left); Adobe Stock, pp. 5 (top), 10 (top left, middle left, bottom left, bottom right), 11 (top right, middle right), 32 (right), 35, 36, 42 (locker photo bottom), 43 (bottom), 44–45 (background), 46–47 (background), 50–51 (background), 51 (top), 57, 61 (all); AP Images, p. 8; Fairchild Archive/Getty Images, p. 55 (all); Hollywood Press Syndicate/Wikimedia Commons, p. 9 (right); Jack Delano/Wikimedia Commons, p. 9 (left); Library of Congress, p. 6 (bottom right); Mighty Media, Inc. (project photos), pp. 50, 51; Rama/Wikimedia Commons, p. 6 (top); Shutterstock Images, pp. 3, 4, 5 (bottom), 10 (top right), 11 (top left, bottom right), 12 (all), 13 (all), 14 (all), 15 (all), 16 (all), 17 (all), 18, 19, 20 (all), 21 (all), 22, 23 (all), 24 (all), 25, 26 (all), 27 (all), 28 (all), 29, 30 (all), 31 (all), 32 (left), 33, 34, 37 (all), 38 (all), 39, 40 (all), 41 (all), 42 (locker, locker photo top and middle), 42–43 (background), 43 (top, middle), 44 (left, right), 46 (left, right), 47 (bottom), 48 (all), 49 (all), 52, 53, 54, 56, 58 (all), 59, 60; Wikimedia Commons, p. 7

Design Elements: Adobe Stock (eyelash texture, hair texture, makeup texture, Polaroid frame, sticky notes, tacks)

Library of Congress Control Number: 2024938317

PUBLISHER'S CATALOGING-IN-PUBLICATION DATA

Names: Gates, Margo, author.
Title: Become a cosmetologist: hairstyling, skin care & more / by Margo Gates
Other Title: hairstyling, skin care & more
Description: Minneapolis, Minnesota : ABDO Publishing, 2025 | Series: Talent to trade | Includes online resources and index.
Identifiers: ISBN 9781098294960 (lib. bdg.) | ISBN 9798384915010 (ebook)
Subjects: LCSH: Cosmetologists--Juvenile literature. | Beauticians--Juvenile literature. | Hair stylists--Juvenile literature. | Makeup artists--Juvenile literature. | Electrologists--Juvenile literature. | Jobs--Juvenile literature. | Trades--Juvenile literature.
Classification: DDC 646.72--dc23

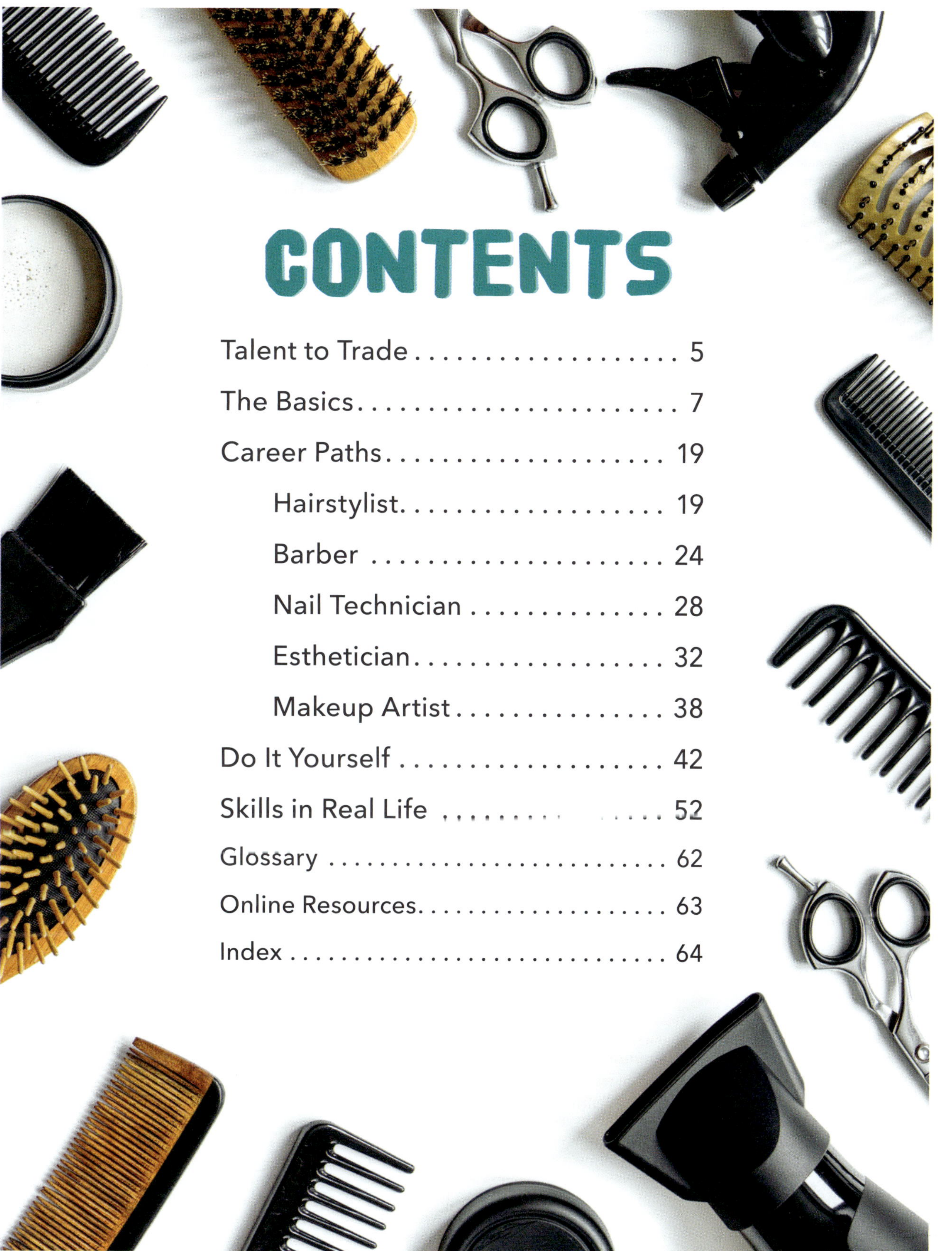

CONTENTS

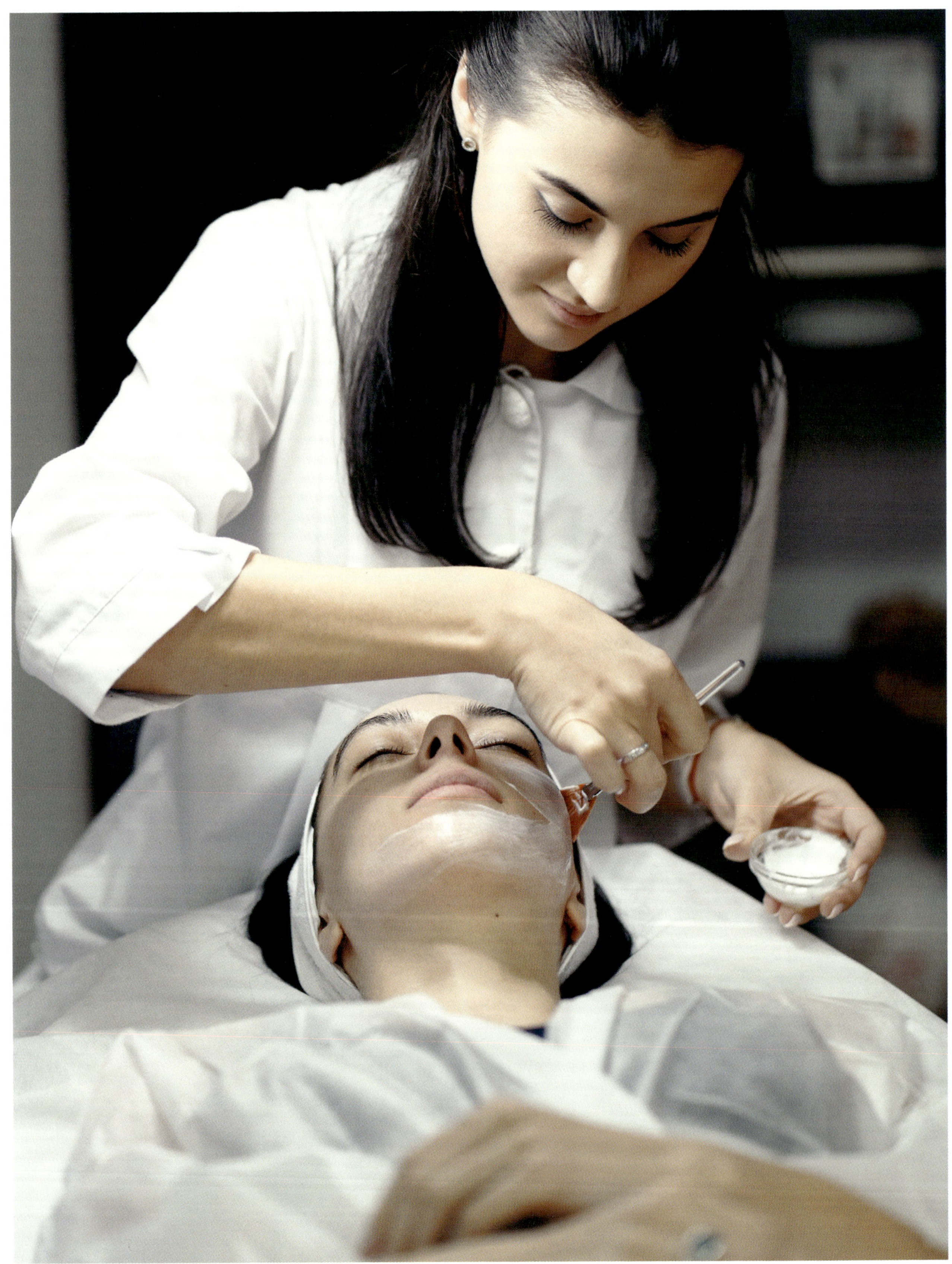

TALENT TO TRADE

Are you fascinated by how cosmetics can transform a person's face? Do you love to watch hairstyling tutorials and practice the techniques you learn? Can you see yourself pampering clients with luxurious pedicures or relaxing facials? If your answer to any of these questions is yes, you might be suited to a career as a cosmetologist. This is a person who provides cosmetic treatments to the hair, nails, and skin.

Becoming a cosmetologist includes a lot of training and hard work. It takes a dedication to mastering techniques, following beauty trends, and caring for clients. But if you have a passion for cosmetology, you may find that the dedication comes naturally and the hard work is worthwhile.

In this book, you'll learn about the history of cosmetology and various jobs in the industry. You'll become familiar with some basic tools, skills, and techniques used by hair, nail, and skin specialists. You'll find inspiration to begin working toward your own career in cosmetology. Finally, you'll learn about some of the ways you can turn your talents into a trade.

Ancient Egyptians used kohl spoons (*pictured*) to store, mix, and use different cosmetic materials.

Madam C.J. Walker's method was known as the "Walker System." It included multiple hair products, lots of brushing, and iron combs.

Martha Matilda Harper created her own hair products. She believed other products had harmful chemicals.

COSMETOLOGY THROUGH THE AGES

Beauty rituals date back to ancient civilizations. Ancient Egyptians lined their eyes with kohl, a black pigment made with ground lead sulfide. For softer skin, they bathed in milk and exfoliated with salt. Ancient Mesopotamians colored their lips using crushed red rocks. Ancient Greeks and Persians curled their hair with bronze tongs heated over a fire. And in ancient China, people colored their nails using dyes from flower petals.

Although beauty practices evolved over centuries, the term cosmetology was first recorded in the 1850s. In the United States, the following century brought the establishment of schools and services relating to hair, nail, and skin care.

In 1891, Canadian-born entrepreneur Martha Matilda Harper started the first US franchise system of hair salons. She taught her beauty methods to the owner of each of her salons. Harper was also an inventor. She developed her own hair tonic and the first reclining shampoo chair.

Another important figure in the history of hair care was Black entrepreneur Madam C.J. Walker. She created a cleansing tonic to address her own hair loss caused by scalp disease. The tonic helped heal her scalp, so Walker began selling it. In 1906, she started a beauty company. Her company eventually made her the first Black woman to become a millionaire. She also established beauty schools that taught her hair care methods.

In 1910, Walker built a factory in Indianapolis, Indiana, to manufacture her miracle hair grower.

The rise of barbershops also has an important place in Black history. During the nation's early years, enslaved men had to provide barbering services for white enslavers. After slavery was outlawed, many Black men opened their own barbershops. In the early 1930s, Henry Miller Morgan opened the nation's first barber college for Black students. It became a national chain that trained many of the country's Black barbers. Over time, barbershops also became meeting hubs in Black communities.

Meanwhile, the professional skin care industry in the US was built in large part by Romanian immigrant Christine Valmy. She had run a skin care salon in Bucharest, Romania. Valmy moved to New York in 1961. She soon discovered that there was a need for specialists who could treat the skin beyond covering it with makeup. In 1966, she opened

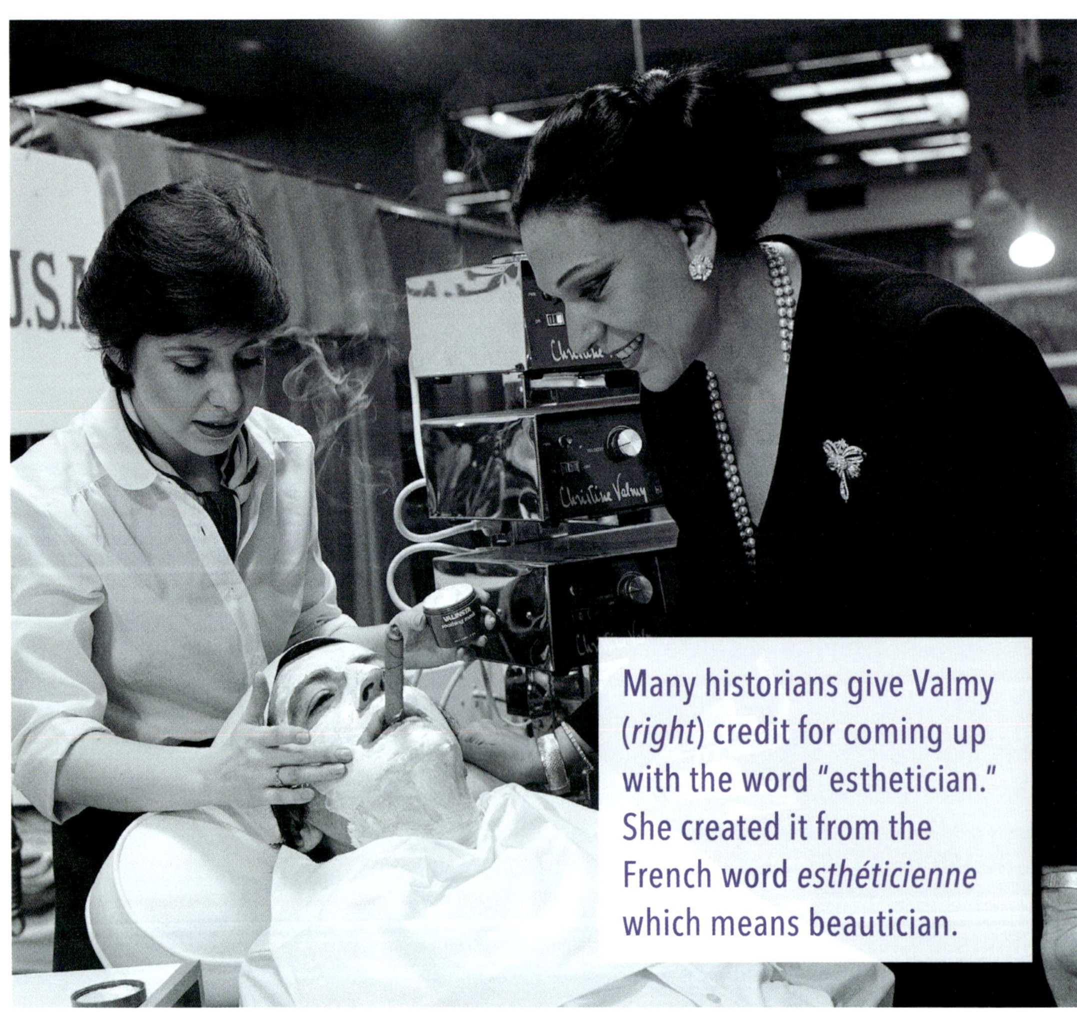

Many historians give Valmy (*right*) credit for coming up with the word "esthetician." She created it from the French word *esthéticienne* which means beautician.

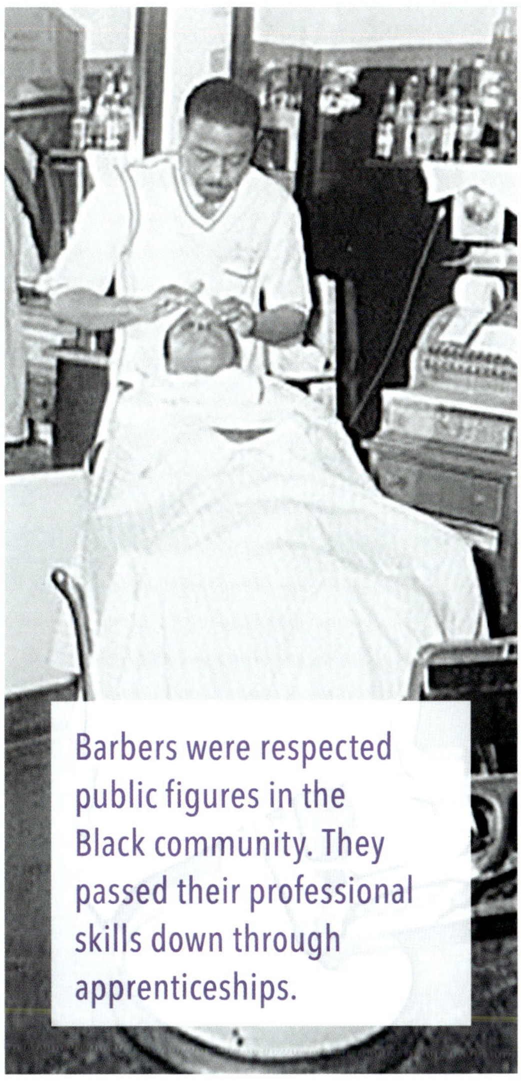

Barbers were respected public figures in the Black community. They passed their professional skills down through apprenticeships.

After visiting a refugee camp in California, movie star Tippi Hedren introduced manicuring to 20 Vietnamese women.

a school where she taught some of the nation's first professional skin care experts.

Immigrants also largely shaped the history of US nail salons. Vietnamese refugees arrived in California in the 1970s. They received training in various trades, including manicuring. Some of them went on to open nail salons. The salons they opened were later passed down through the generations.

Today, the nation's beauty service market generates billions of dollars in revenue each year. In the following pages, you'll learn what it takes to work as a professional in this industry. You may even be inspired to start your journey to becoming a cosmetologist!

TOOLS OF THE TRADE

Get familiar with some of the tools specialists use to improve the health and beauty of hair, nails, and skin.

HAIR

CAPES

Hairstylists and barbers use capes to cover their clients' skin and clothing. Capes protect clients from hair clippings, water, and dyes or other chemicals used on the hair. Capes attach and fit snuggly around the neck, draping loosely over the client's arms and torso.

COMBS & BRUSHES

Stylists use combs and brushes to detangle, smooth out, and style hair. Often, stylists use combs on wet hair and brushes on dry hair. Combs and brushes come in a variety of forms. Each comb or brush shape suits a specific hair type or performs a specific task. For example, a cutting comb keeps hair taut and even as the stylist cuts it. A round brush is often used with a blow dryer to give the hair volume.

SHEARS

Cutting shears have two straight blades whose sharp edges come together to cut through hair. Stylists can choose from a variety of styles and blade lengths based on their cutting technique. Some cutting shears, known as thinning shears, have one straight blade while the other blade has comb-like teeth. When the two blades come together, only a portion of the hair between them is cut. Stylists use thinning shears to thin out thicker hair or to add texture to hair.

CLIPPERS & TRIMMERS

Clippers are electric devices that stylists and barbers use for shorter haircuts. Stylists often use clipper attachments called guide combs. This makes it easy for stylists to cut hair to a certain length. Trimmers are similar to clippers, but they cut hair closer to the skin. They help barbers and stylists clean up beards and sideburns.

SHAVERS & RAZORS

Shavers are electric devices that barbers use to efficiently shave a client's facial hair. A shaver's blade doesn't make direct contact with the skin. This helps prevent cuts and irritation. Straight razors provide cleaner, closer shaves than electric shavers. But they require more time and skill to use. This is because a straight razor's blade touches skin directly.

COLOR BAR

Many salons that offer hair coloring services have a color bar. This is a station where hair dyes are stored and mixed to create custom hair colors. Color bars also house other hair coloring supplies. This can include gloves, foil, clips, brushes, and more.

HAIR DRYERS

Stylists dry and style hair using hooded or handheld hair dryers. There are two different types of hooded dryers. The first has a soft cap that fits snuggly around the scalp. The second has a hard dome that surrounds the client's head. Hooded dryers diffuse heat evenly around the scalp. They also aid in the absorption of product into the hair. Stylists often use them on curly-haired clients who want their hair held in place. Meanwhile, handheld hair dryers deliver a more concentrated heat to one section of hair at a time. Stylists often use them on clients who want a more free-flowing hairstyle.

CURLING & FLAT IRONS

Curling irons and flat irons are tools that use heat to style hair. A stylist wraps a section of hair around the rod-shaped curling iron to create curls. Meanwhile, a flat iron has two flat plates that clamp onto a section of hair. The stylist moves the clamped plates down the length of the hair to smooth and straighten the hair. Using a different technique, stylists can also create waves or curls using a flat iron.

NAILS

NAIL SHAPING

Nail technicians use clippers to shorten longer nails. Then they use files to shape the nails and smooth the edges. Buffer blocks make the surface of the nail smooth and shiny. Some nail techs may use electric rotary tools called nail drills. Drills file and buff nails as well as remove acrylic and gel nails.

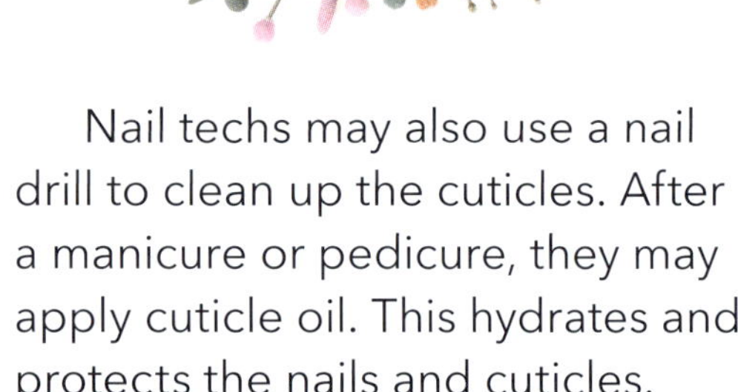

Nail techs may also use a nail drill to clean up the cuticles. After a manicure or pedicure, they may apply cuticle oil. This hydrates and protects the nails and cuticles.

CUTICLE CARE

Every nail has a thin layer of dead skin that seals off the base of the nail called a cuticle. The cuticle protects the nail from germs. Proper cuticle grooming improves nail health. It also enhances the nail's appearance and prepares it for polish. Nail techs first soften clients' cuticles in warm water. Then they gently push the cuticles off the nail using a cuticle pusher.

NAIL EXTENSIONS

Nail techs use a variety of materials to artificially extend nails. This may include plastic tips, silk fabric, or thin layers of fiberglass. Nail techs attach these materials to the natural nail with adhesives. They might also use nail forms. A nail form fits snuggly beneath the nail. This creates a temporary base to build a gel or acrylic nail. Once the nail is built up to the desired length and dried, the nail form is removed.

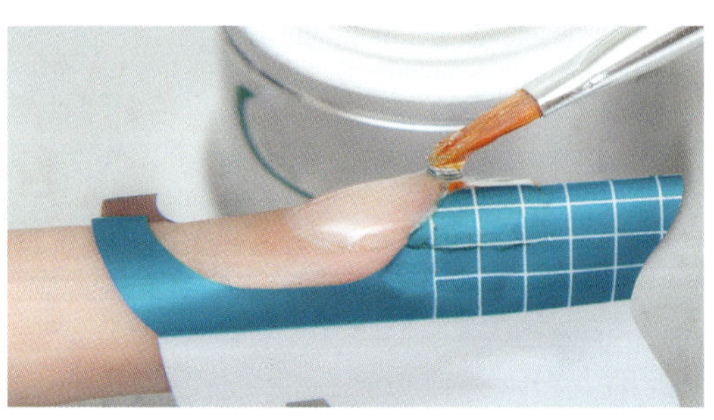

NAIL POLISH

There are several types of polish that clients can choose from. This includes traditional nail polish, gel nail polish, and acrylic. Traditional nail polish brushes onto the nail in thin layers. It is the quickest to apply and remove. But it easily chips off the nail. Gel nail polish brushes on nails like traditional polish. But it's dried under a lamp that gives off ultraviolet light which hardens the polish. This creates a glossy finish that lasts longer than traditional polish. Acrylic is a gluelike paste that a nail tech creates by combining a liquid and powder. The tech spreads this thick paste over the nail with a brush. It then dries into a hard, strong layer of polish.

NAIL DUST PROTECTION

Nail dust collectors are ventilation devices. They suck up tiny particles sent into the air by nail files and drills. This prevents nail techs and their clients from breathing in these particles. Many nail techs wear face masks, gloves, and protective glasses. This also helps protect them from nail dust.

FOOT SPA

Many nail salons have footbaths that clients soak their feet in during pedicures. These warm-water baths clean and soften the skin of the feet. They often have jets that gently massage the feet. Some nail salons have footbaths that are connected to massage chairs. This provides an even more relaxing pedicure experience.

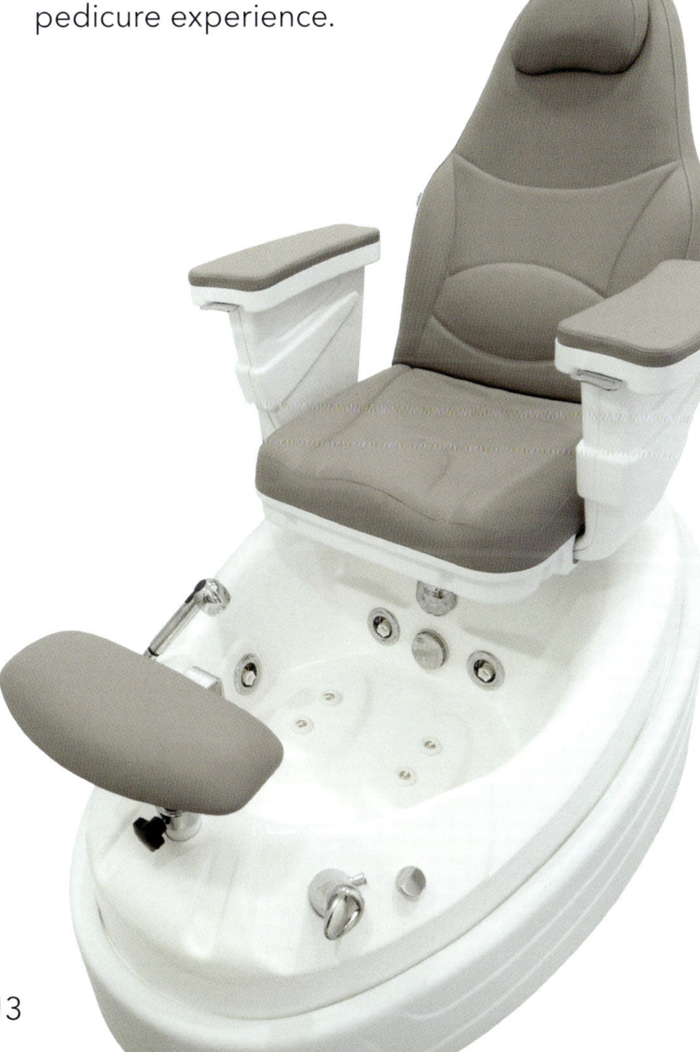

SKIN

MAGNIFICATION LAMP

A magnification lamp lights up and magnifies the facial skin. This allows skin care specialists to closely inspect the client's pores and analyze their skin.

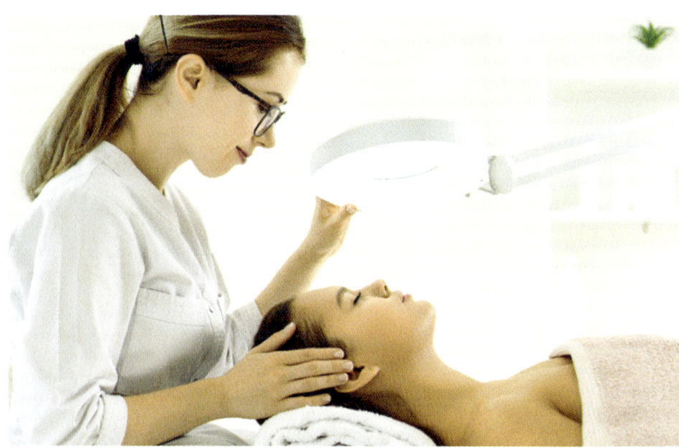

FACIAL STEAMER

A facial steamer is a device that heats water into steam. It then blows the steam toward a client's face. Skin care specialists use this tool to soften the client's skin. This makes it easier to remove any debris clogging the pores.

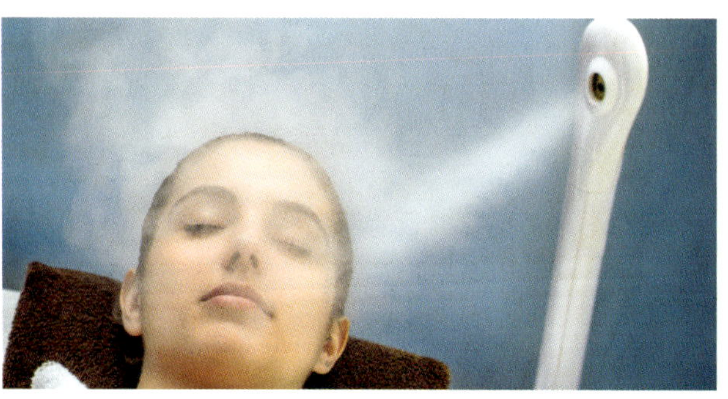

EXFOLIATING TOOLS

Skin specialists use a variety of tools to remove dead skin cells from the skin's surface. This process is called exfoliation. It prevents dead skin cells from clogging pores. It also helps the skin absorb skin care products. Handheld brushes are basic exfoliating tools. More advanced tools include microdermabrasion machines and ultrasonic skin scrubbers.

HAIR REMOVAL TOOLS

Skin care specialists use a variety of materials to remove facial and body hair. Tweezers grab and pull out individual hairs. Twisted cotton thread can pull out multiple hairs at a time. Wax pulls out larger areas of hair in one swift motion.

PRIMER & FOUNDATION

Before applying most cosmetics, makeup artists often begin with a base of primer and foundation. Primer is a cream or gel that fills in fine lines, wrinkles, and pores. This creates a smooth surface for the foundation to

bond with. Foundation is makeup that matches a person's natural skin tone. It is applied all over the face to create a uniform complexion. Foundation comes in several forms, including creams, sticks, and powders.

BLUSHES, BRONZERS & HIGHLIGHTERS

Makeup artists can give their clients a radiant look with blush, bronzer, and highlighter. Blush is applied to the cheeks. It creates a naturally flushed color. Bronzer is applied all over or in specific areas. It gives the face a sun-kissed glow. And highlighter brings brightness to the face's high points. This includes the bridge of the nose and the cheekbones.

EYES & LIPS

Makeup artists use various cosmetics to draw attention to a client's features. Eyeshadow adds natural depth and dimension or a bold pop of color to the eyes. Eyeliner helps define the eyes. Mascara makes the eyelashes appear darker, thicker, and longer. Makeup artists draw attention to the lips using lipstick or lip gloss. Lip liner makes lips appear fuller and prevents lipstick from smudging.

SPECIAL EFFECTS MAKEUP

Some makeup artists specialize in applying makeup to create an illusion or drastically alter a person's face. Special effects makeup artists create their looks with different materials. This includes prosthetics, adhesives, fake blood, airbrush equipment, and more.

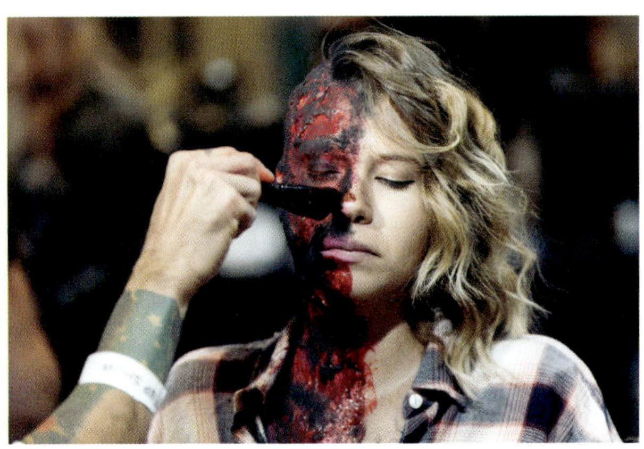

SPECIAL SKILLS

Explore some of the skills that hair, nail, and skin specialists need to do their jobs.

ATTENTION TO DETAIL

Nail technicians must uniformly shape nails and make nail extensions appear natural. Makeup artists must match foundation to their client's skin tone. Skin care specialists must examine a client's skin type to determine which products or methods to use.

CREATIVITY

Many clients ask cosmetologists to create something fun and different. This can be a funky new hairstyle, an edgy makeup look, or some flashy nail art. Cosmetologists must be ready to get creative on the spot!

COMMUNICATION

A cosmetologist must listen closely to understand their client's vision. They should be able to clearly explain the steps of a treatment or process to prepare their client. They must also observe nonverbal cues to perceive if a client is uncertain or uncomfortable.

CUSTOMER CARE

Cosmetologists are skilled at making sure their clients feel comfortable. A hairstylist makes sure they are using the right amount of pressure while giving a scalp massage. A nail technician ensures their client's footbath is not too hot. And a barber may use essential oil on a hot facial towel to help their client relax.

DEXTERITY

A hairstylist must swiftly and skillfully move their comb and shears around a client's head without accidently poking them. A barber must shave a client's face with a sharp razor without cutting them. A skin care specialist uses a thin thread to pull tiny hairs from a client's eyebrows. These and many other tasks require great manual dexterity and coordination.

ORGANIZATION

Cosmetologists must keep their workstations tidy, storing all their tools in drawers, kits, or cases for easy access. Proper organization allows cosmetologists to work efficiently while keeping their tools clean and well-stocked.

STAMINA

Besides being on their feet for hours at a time, cosmetologists must perform repetitive motions, such as twisting a curling iron or filing nails. They might also have to hold less comfortable positions, such as bending over a wash basin to wash clients' hair. These motions and positions can put stress on the joints. Cosmetologists must have stamina and proper technique to perform these actions daily without causing injury.

TIME MANAGEMENT

Staying on schedule is essential for cosmetologists because falling behind with one client means being late for the next. Since most services offered by hair, nail, and skin specialists involve multiple steps, these professionals must also be mindful of the amount of time spent on each step. Time management is also vital for any process involving chemicals, such as hair bleaching or texturizing. Prolonged exposure to chemicals can cause excessive damage to a client's hair.

CAREERS IN COSMETOLOGY

Cosmetologists are trained to provide services in hairstyling, nail care, skin care, and makeup. However, many cosmetologists choose to specialize in one of these areas. Let's explore some career paths for those interested in cosmetology!

HAIRSTYLIST

Many hairstylists work in salons, where they provide a variety of hair services to clients.

CONSULTING

A hairstylist often begins a client appointment with a consultation. The client describes their goals and may also ask the stylist for an opinion. It's the stylist's job to understand what the client is looking for and suggest a plan of action. The stylist may also make style or color recommendations. They base these on the client's face shape, skin tone, or other factors. A good hairstylist also knows how to listen closely and communicate their thoughts clearly during a consultation.

Sometimes an assistant washes a client's hair before it's cut by the hairstylist. This gives the hairstylist time to work on more clients during the day.

Most hairstylists see about 6 to 20 clients a day.

HAIR & SCALP CARE

A client may choose to have their hair and scalp washed at the start of their appointment. A stylist may choose between different shampoos, conditioners, and other products. They base their decision on the client's hair type and scalp condition. During the wash, stylists often provide a scalp massage. This helps the client relax and can also stimulate hair growth. This part of a hair service requires stylists to be dexterous and perceptive to the client's comfort level.

CUT & STYLE

Some clients may request a hair trim. Trims remove the damaged ends while maintaining the hair's general length and style. Other clients may request more drastic changes in length or style. A hairstylist must decide which cutting and styling tools will help them achieve the requested hairstyle.

COLOR & BLEACH

Hairstylists also help clients who want to change their hair color. This involves applying a dye to achieve a new color or applying bleach. The bleach lifts color from the hair, achieving a lighter color. Clients may choose to color their entire head of hair or just certain sections of it. For example, a stylist adds highlights to hair by separating out and bleaching or dyeing small sections of it. When coloring hair, stylists must work efficiently and be conscious of time. Leaving dye or bleach on hair for too much or too little time will affect the final color. It can also cause excessive damage to their client's hair.

CHEMICAL TREATMENTS

Clients also go to salons to change their hair texture. These treatments use chemicals that break the bonds in hair. It also resets hair in a new shape. Chemicals that make curly hair straight are called relaxers. Those that make curls looser and smoother are called texturizers. And a chemical treatment that makes straight hair curly is called a perm. Because these treatments use chemicals, stylists must pay close attention to timing and proper procedure. This helps them avoid excessive damage to hair.

EXTENSIONS

Some salons offer hair extension services for clients who want their hair to appear longer or fuller. Hair extensions are sections of real or synthetic hair that are incorporated into a client's natural hair. Stylists use various methods to apply extensions. In one method, a stylist threads sections of natural hair through small beads called microbeads. They feed an extension through each bead. Stylists clamp the beads with pliers, binding extensions to natural hair. Extensions can take several hours to apply. Stylists must maintain their focus and attention to detail throughout the entire process!

A hairstylist usually creates a perm, or a permanent wave, by wrapping their client's hair in rods and applying a chemical solution to keep the hair in place.

Hairstylists need a special certification before providing hair extension services. To get the certification, they need to learn how to install, remove, maintain, and care for extensions.

BARBER

Barbers often work in barbershops or salons. They provide many of the same services as hairstylists, but focus on short hairstyles and various facial grooming services.

FACIAL HAIR MAINTENANCE

Barbers use combs, shears, clippers, and trimmers to help clients maintain their beards and mustaches. They apply oils and waxes to moisturize facial hair and skin. A barber may also recommend flattering beard and mustache shapes based on a client's face shape and features.

Though most people can shave their own beards, barbers are able to create a cleaner and more professional look.

A barber must maintain precise control of the razor with a steady hand. This ensures a relaxing, safe shave for the client.

Waxing provides many benefits, including smoother skin and fewer ingrown hairs.

SHAVING

A close shave is a long-standing barbershop tradition. Barbers offer this service as an opportunity to pamper clients. A barber starts by applying a moist, hot towel to their client's face. This prepares the skin for shaving and softens facial hair, making it easier to cut. Then the barber applies a warm lather to the skin to further relax the hair before shaving it. Many barbers shave with a straight razor. This is a sharp blade that folds into its handle. Often, the shave service ends with a cool towel wrapped around the face to soothe and tighten the skin.

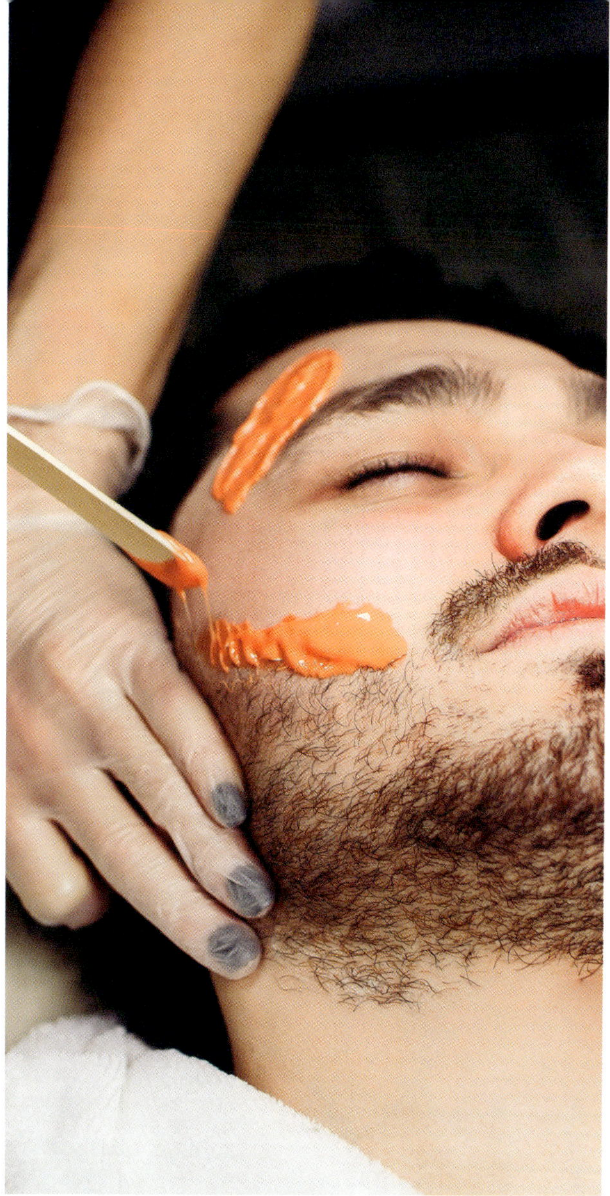

WAXING

In addition to maintaining clients' beards and mustaches, many barbers also provide waxing services. This service removes unwanted eyebrow, nose, and ear hair. To do this, a barber applies a warm wax to the skin around a client's eyebrows or just inside their nostrils or ears. Once the wax has hardened around the hairs, the barber swiftly removes it from the skin, pulling the hairs off with it.

NAIL TECHNICIAN

Nail technicians groom and beautify clients' fingernails and toenails. This work takes patience, precision, and focus. Many of these specialists work at nail salons. But full-service beauty salons and spas also employ nail techs.

MANI & PEDI

A manicure is a cosmetic treatment of the hands and fingernails. A pedicure is a similar treatment done on the feet and toenails. For these services, a nail tech trims, files, and buffs the client's nails. They use gels or creams to soften the skin around the nail. This makes it easier to clean and trim cuticles. Manicures and pedicures often include an exfoliating scrub. This helps remove dead skin cells. Then the nail tech will provide a moisturizing hand or foot massage. In the final part of the service, the tech finishes the nails with polish.

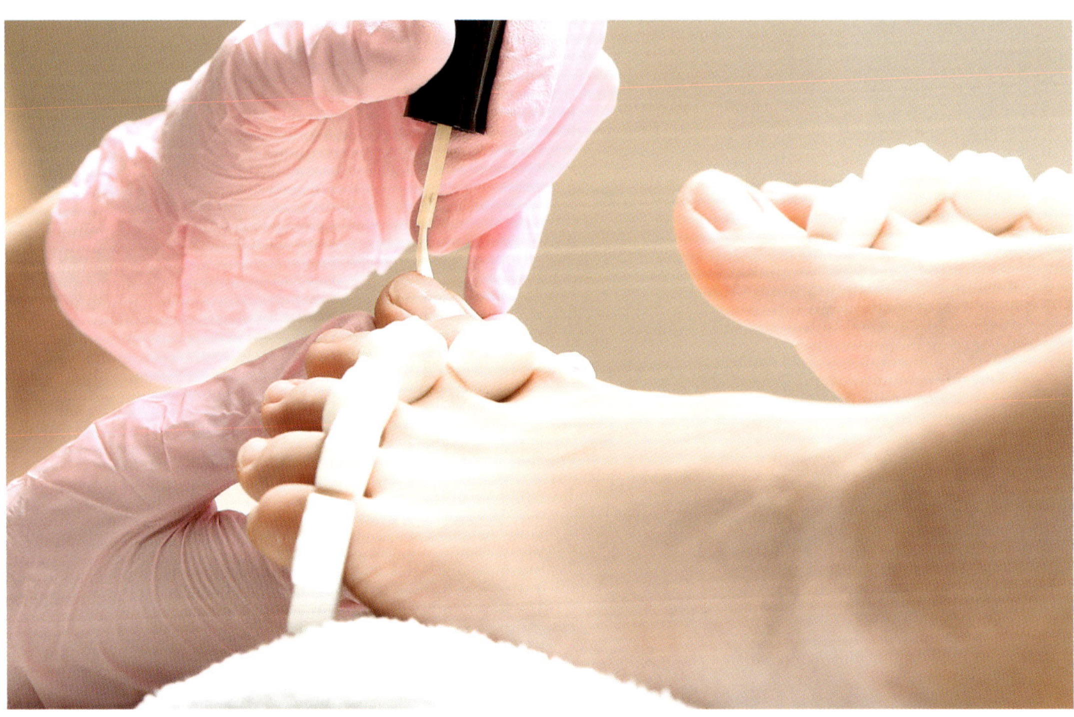

Many salons offer multiple nail care packages. More expensive packages have benefits such as a longer massage or a pampering skin treatment. Skin treatments may include using an exfoliating scrub or applying a skin-softening wax.

Some nail salons have examples of the art they can create. Clients can also show their nail tech photos of the types of nail art they want.

Many nail salons offer a nail fill service. Clients can return after a few weeks and get the space between their cuticles and the nail extensions refilled.

NAIL EXTENSIONS

While some clients simply have their natural nails polished, others choose to have their nails artificially extended first. Extensions are adhered to the natural nail and hardened. Then they are shaped, smoothed, and polished.

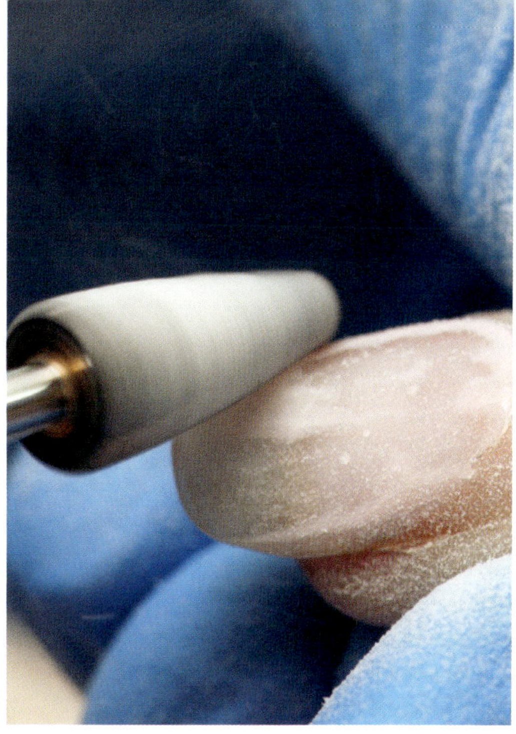

NAIL ART

Many people like to express themselves with fun nail art. Nail art is any design, pattern, or embellishment beyond a solid coat of polish. This includes glitter, rhinestones, stickers, metallic foils, and more. Most nail technicians can provide basic nail art services. But painting intricate patterns and designs is a specialty that only some nail techs offer.

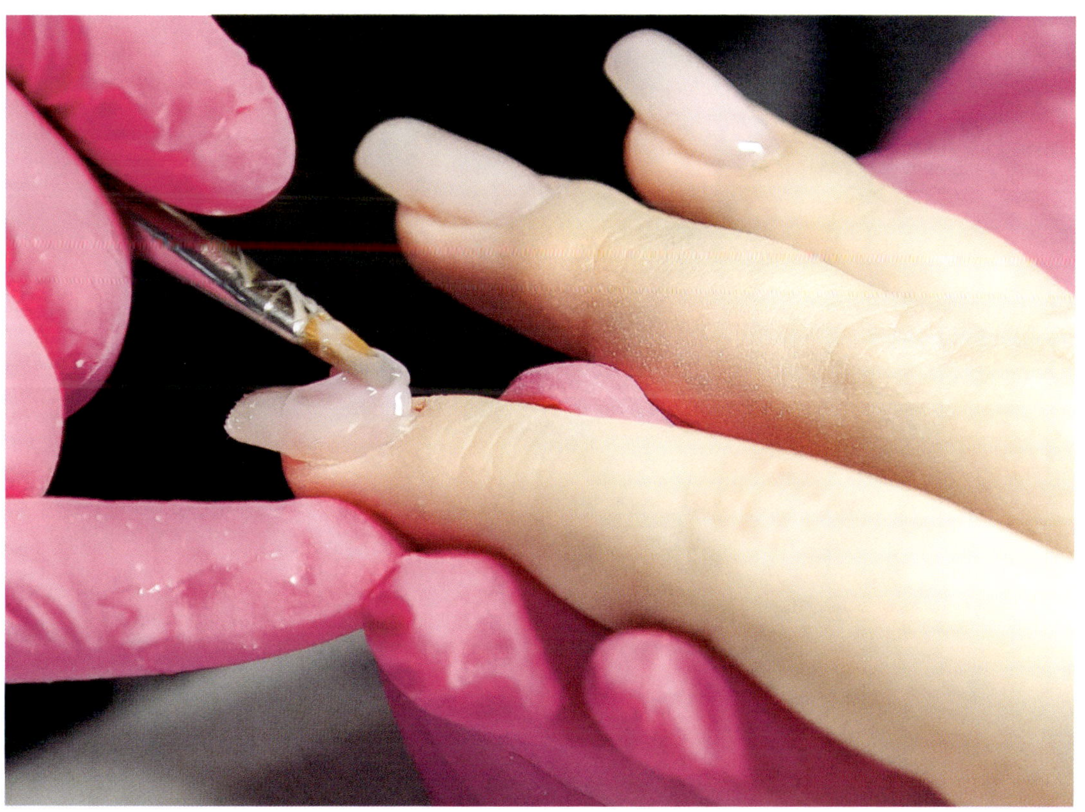

ESTHETICIAN

An esthetician is a skin care specialist who provides skin treatments and recommendations. Their goal is to enhance the health and appearance of their clients' skin. Many estheticians work at salons and spas. Some provide skin treatments at dermatology clinics or other medical establishments.

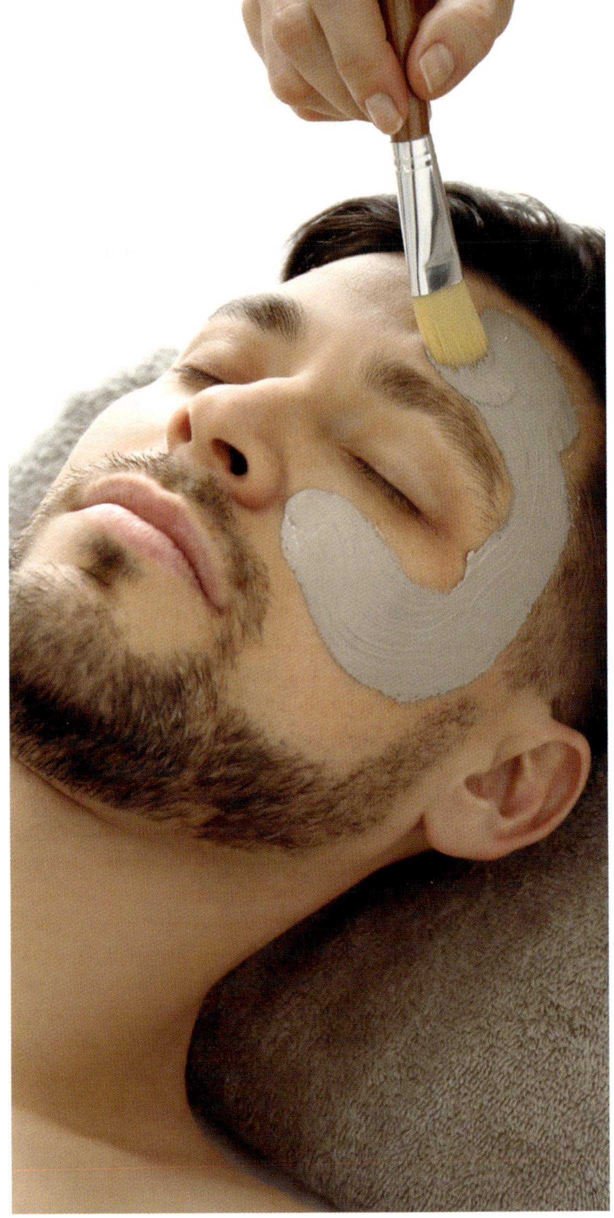

SKIN ANALYSIS

An appointment with an esthetician begins with a skin analysis. The specialist determines the client's skin type, such as dry, oily, or sensitive. They also determine if the client has any skin conditions. This can include acne, rosacea, or eczema. The esthetician will then suggest treatment options that are suited to the client's skin type and conditions. They may also suggest skin care products the client should use or avoid.

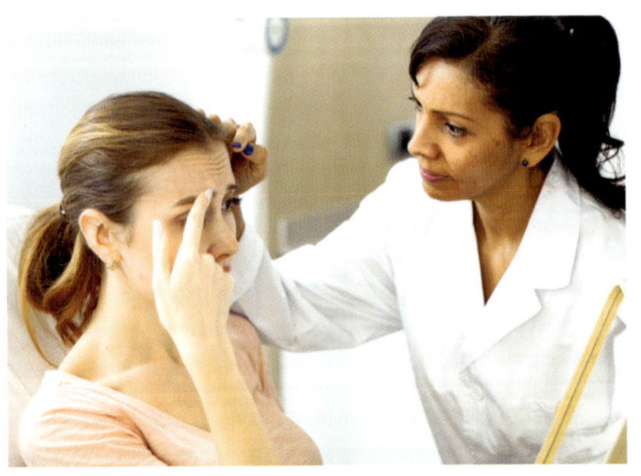

FACIALS

A facial is a relaxing treatment that improves the health and appearance of the facial skin. A typical facial treatment includes cleansing and exfoliating. It also includes moisturizing the skin using products such as cream masks, serums, and oils. However, an esthetician must tailor their process and the products they use to the client's skin type and conditions.

Most facials include a massage which helps to relax clients and refresh their skin and facial muscles.

Some estheticians offer special treatments to help tighten sagging skin, giving it a firmer and more youthful look.

SKIN TREATMENTS

In addition to basic facial services, estheticians can also offer more specialized skin treatments. This can include microdermabrasion, chemical peels, microneedling, and laser resurfacing.

Microdermabrasion is a procedure that removes damaged or dead skin cells. It uses superfine crystals or a diamond-tipped wand. The result is a smoother, more even complexion.

A light chemical peel is a treatment that uses a mildly acidic solution. This removes the outermost layer of skin. It helps reveal new and smoother skin.

Microneedling is the practice of using tiny needles to puncture the skin. It stimulates the production of proteins. This makes the skin firm and smooth.

Laser resurfacing has a similar effect as microneedling, but it uses lasers instead of needles. The lasers remove the outer layer of skin. It also stimulates the production of proteins, resulting in new skin growth.

The use of chemicals, needles, or lasers by estheticians is often limited by state laws. For example, in many states, estheticians can only do certain procedures under the supervision of a medical professional.

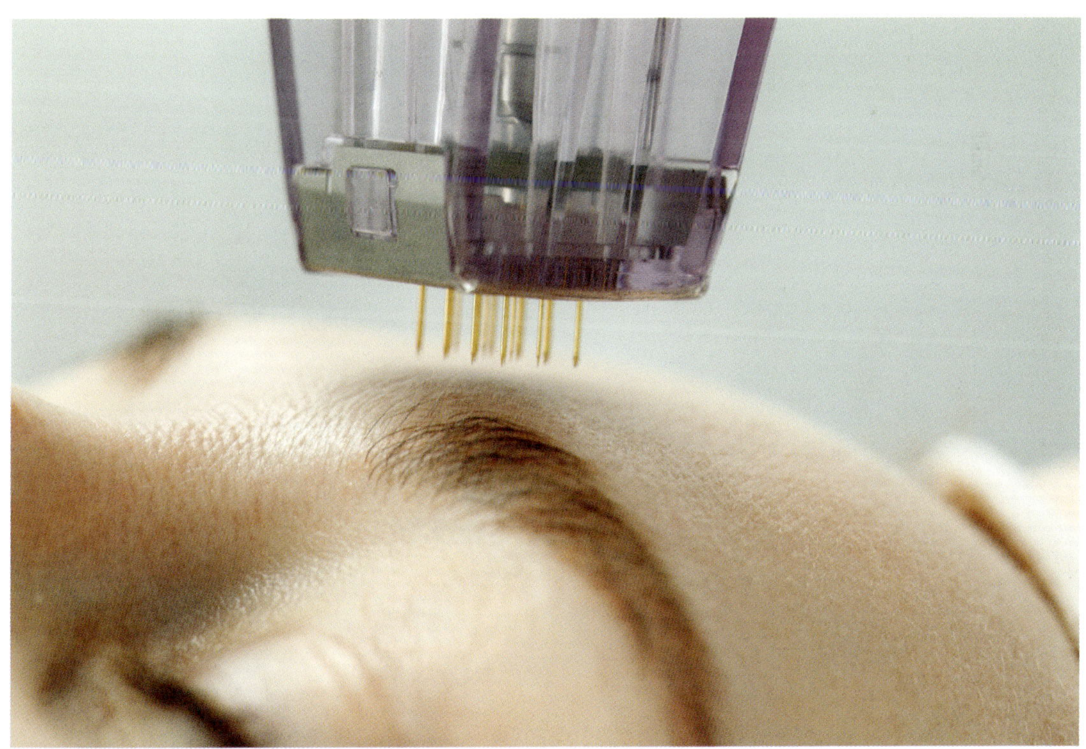

BODY TREATMENTS

In addition to facial treatments, estheticians offer a range of full-body treatments. These treatments rejuvenate the skin of the torso and limbs. A scrub is a treatment that removes debris and dead cells from the surface of the skin. A scrub uses exfoliants such as salt or sugar. An esthetician massages the exfoliant into the skin. This clears clogged pores, stimulates blood flow, and more.

Another body treatment is a mask or wrap. The treatment may begin with an exfoliating scrub. Next, the esthetician covers the client's torso and limbs with a mask made of natural substances. This can include mud, clay, or seaweed. Then the esthetician wraps the client's body in cotton, plastic film, or another material. The wrap traps moisture and heat against the body. This helps cleanse, soften, and moisturize the skin.

HAIR REMOVAL

Skin contains follicles from which hair grows. As skin specialists, estheticians are experts in facial and body hair along with the various methods of removing it. Threading is a common technique for removing facial hair and shaping eyebrows. It is done by gliding a thin, twisted thread over the skin. The thread catches the hair and pulls it from the follicle.

Waxing and sugaring are other methods that pull hair from the follicle. They are used for both facial and body hair. Wax is spread over hair in the same direction that it grows. It's then pulled off in the opposite direction. Sugaring uses a paste of sugar, lemon, and water. It is applied to the skin in the opposite direction of hair growth. Then it is pulled off in the same direction the hair grows.

Some estheticians receive additional training to provide more specialized hair removal services. This includes laser hair removal or electrolysis. Both of these methods damage the hair follicles to slow down or stop hair growth. Laser hair removal does this with mild radiation while electrolysis uses electric currents. As is the case with certain skin treatments, estheticians in many states can only provide these services if they are supervised by medical professionals.

Scrubs (*pictured*) help to hydrate the skin, improve skin texture, and prevent ingrown hairs. Body wraps help to improve blood circulation, lessen stretch marks, and relax the client.

Laser hair removal permanently removes unwanted hair after multiple sessions.

MAKEUP ARTIST

Makeup artists are experts at skillfully applying cosmetics. Their goal is to achieve a specific look or effect. These specialists work in a wide variety of settings. This can be anywhere from salons to cosmetic companies to department store makeup counters. Some makeup artists work in the same setting every day. Others travel to do makeup for special events. These can be weddings, fashion shows, and photo shoots. Depending on their workplace or clients, makeup artists may specialize in certain makeup techniques and looks. Whatever their specialty, a good makeup artist has a sharp eye for color and detail.

NATURAL

Artists who work with customers at cosmetic stores or do makeup for weddings are often asked to create natural makeup looks. This look uses minimal product. It highlights a client's natural beauty without calling attention to their makeup. When applying this look, a makeup artist must be skilled at choosing cosmetics that blend seamlessly with the client's skin.

GLAMOUR

Glamour makeup creates a bolder look than natural makeup. It typically involves contouring. This technique uses makeup to sculpt the face and better define certain features. Glamour looks are characterized by dramatic eyes that are often accentuated with false eyelashes. Makeup artists may apply this look to models, celebrities, and other clients for commercial photo shoots or formal events.

There are two types of glamour looks. Full glam uses bolder and darker colors to create confident and dramatic looks. Soft glam (*pictured*) is a blend of natural and full glam.

High fashion makeup artists must work together with fashion designers, hairstylists, and models. This helps to create a seamless look that blends well with the model's hair, clothes, and accessories.

Production makeup that completely changes a person's look can take several hours to apply.

HIGH FASHION

Fashion shows and other events feature the work of high-end clothing and accessory designers. For these events, makeup artists often create striking, fantastical looks for the models. They may use bold colors and sharp lines. They may also use embellishments such as feathers, pearls, and sequins. These makeup artists must be highly creative. They may also take their inspiration from the fashion designs on display.

STAGE & SCREEN

Some makeup artists do the makeup for actors in theater, film, or TV productions. For a stage production, a makeup artist typically uses heavy makeup to exaggerate an actor's features. This allows viewers farther from the stage to see the actor's expressions. It also prevents the actor from appearing overly pale under the bright stage lights. In comparison, a screen production allows for close-up shots of an actor's face. So a makeup artist will often use a more subtle makeup application. This gives the actor a natural yet unblemished look.

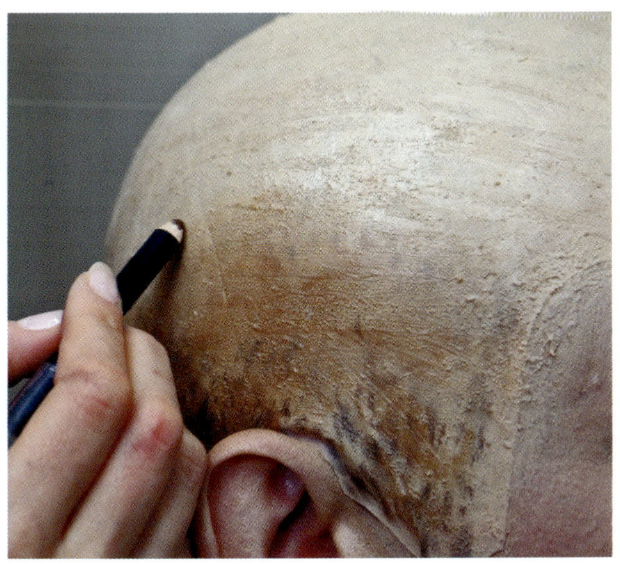

Some makeup artists specialize in special effects makeup for stage or screen productions. A makeup artist may use wax to create a realistic scar or wound across an actor's face. Or, they might use silicone and skin adhesive to make an actor look like a scaly alien. The results can be shocking!

CREATE YOUR VISION

It's time to get creative! Think about your hobbies and interests that relate to cosmetology. Create a vision board that reflects these and whatever else inspires you. Let it motivate you to turn your talents into your trade!

Put your vision board where you'll see it on a regular basis, such as in your locker or next to your bed.

Apply to Cosmetology School

Plan for the future!

Display magazine pages, quotes, and photos that reflect your style and interests.
"Beauty is an attitude."
—Estee Lauder

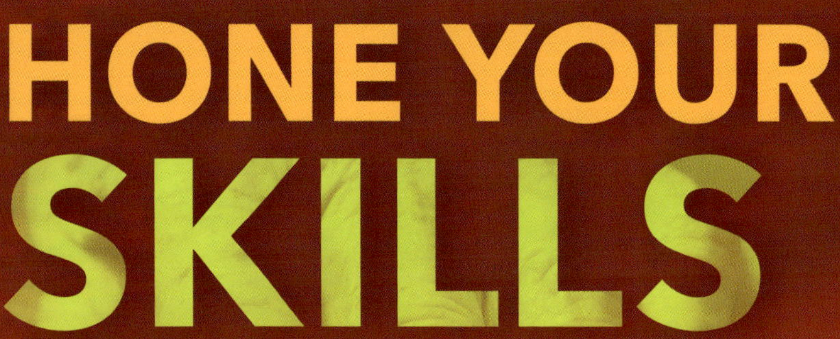

HONE YOUR SKILLS

You've got the passion, vision, and motivation. Even if you aren't ready to start formal training, you can still take steps to develop and grow your skills!

Use inexpensive wigs to practice cutting hair.

Host a spa day for your friends and practice applying face masks or other skin care techniques.

Volunteer
to paint nails
at a local
senior living
facility.

SHOWCASE YOUR TALENTS

As you develop your skills, don't be afraid to show off your work. Doing so will help you build confidence. It will also encourage others to support you as you pursue your goals!

Create video tutorials for different hair styles.

Share photos of your nail art on social media.

Start a blog or vlog that rates different skin care products and methods.
Make a podcast discussing recent industry trends.

START YOUR SIDE HUSTLE

Need a little extra cash? Brainstorm ways you can apply your talents to make money. What kinds of side jobs can you create for yourself?

Offer to help do makeup for a community theater production.

Style hair for friends and family for formal dances, parties, or weddings.

Assemble boxes with
your favorite beauty products.
Sell them for a small profit or
donate to a local charity!

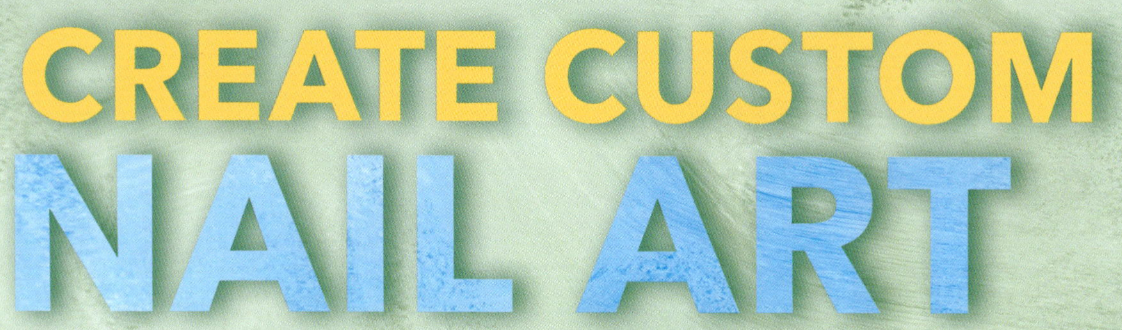

CREATE CUSTOM NAIL ART

A fun way to experiment with nail art is to try out different designs on press-on nail samples. Share your finished designs with friends or future clients!

Tip!

Soak your finished nails in ice water. This will help them set faster.

SUPPLIES

press-on nails
gel nail polish (various colors)
toothpicks
clear nail polish

STEPS

1 Paint the nails with two coats of light blue polish. Let the polish dry between coats.

2 Once the polish is dry, brush two to three small circles of white polish near each other on one nail.

3 Dip the tip of a toothpick in the white polish. Use the tip to connect the circles into a fluffy cloud shape.

4 Repeat steps 2 and 3 with the remaining nails. Try adding at least two clouds per nail. The clouds can cut off at the edges of the nail. Let the polish dry.

5 Paint the nails with clear polish and let them dry.

BECOMING A COSMOTOLOGIST

TRAINING

Do you want to know what it takes to be a hair, nail, or skin specialist? For many people, their path begins with cosmetology school, which provides training in hairstyling, nail services, skin care, and makeup.

However, barbers and estheticians provide services that are not taught in cosmetology school, so they typically must receive specialized training. People interested in working only with hair, nails, or makeup can also attend programs specific to those specialties. In some states, students can train through apprenticeships instead of schools or other programs.

After completing training, most hair, nail, and skin specialists must obtain a license to perform services for clients. To obtain a license, they must meet certain education requirements, which vary by state and specialty. They must also pass a licensure exam.

FINDING A JOB

Once you've met the requirements to work in your state, it's time to find a job!

JOB SEARCH TIPS

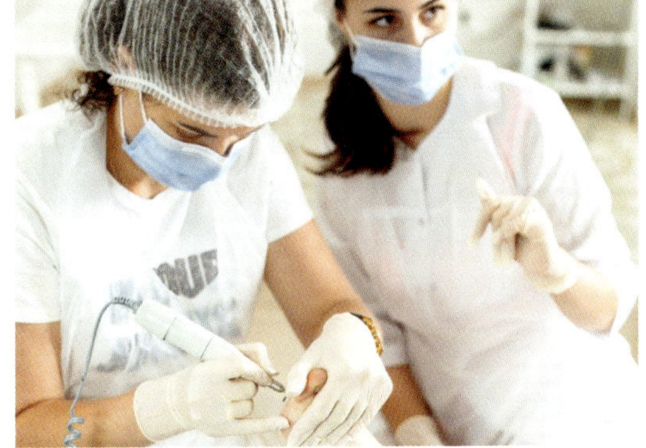

> Create a résumé that outlines your education and training as well as your work history. Even if you have not worked in the industry, highlight any extracurricular experiences in which you applied skills that are relevant to the role you are pursuing. If you have a website, online portfolio, or social media account showcasing your work, include these links in your résumé.

> Keep in regular contact with the instructors and classmates from your training program. Ask them to put you in touch with others in the industry. The goal is to grow your professional network and learn about possible job opportunities.

> Identify salons, barbershops, spas, or other establishments where you would like to work. Introduce yourself to the manager and ask for an informational interview so you can learn more about their business. Express your interest in working there, and leave them with a copy of your résumé.

> If you are invited to interview for a job, be prepared! Before the interview, research the business's history, mission statements, and offerings. Be ready to articulate why you want to work for the business and how you think you'd be a good fit for the role. Finally, have your own questions prepared for the interviewer. This shows you are thoughtful and serious about the job!

> Is there somewhere you really want to work, but there aren't any job openings for the role you're after? Consider applying for a different role, such as an assistant, receptionist, or intern. This tactic is known as "getting your foot in the door." By using this tactic, you'll be in a strong position to be considered for your desired position when it becomes available.

CAREER PROGRESSION

Education doesn't stop once you land your first job. In many states, beauty industry specialists must periodically renew their licenses. Requirements for license renewal often include additional training to learn new techniques or stay up to date on health and safety standards.

Even if additional training isn't required, it's important that beauty specialists seek out professional development opportunities. This might mean taking courses to earn additional certifications, attending industry conferences, or simply watching video tutorials and experimenting with new techniques.

Some states require cosmetologists to complete a certain number of training hours to renew their licenses. In other states, cosmetologists can complete their renewal online without any course requirements.

MEET A PRO: PAT McGRATH, MAKEUP ARTIST

Born in England in 1970, Patricia Ann McGrath was raised by a mother obsessed with beauty and fashion. Growing up, Pat and her mother had trouble finding makeup for dark skin. This ignited Pat's passion for beauty and fashion. As a professional, McGrath worked hard to make fashion more inclusive. In 2015, she launched her own line of cosmetics that are developed for a variety of skin tones. Just three years later, the line was valued at $1 billion! As one of the most influential makeup artists in the fashion industry, McGrath is famous for the bold and experimental looks she creates for fashion shows.

McGrath at the Dolce & Gabbana Fall 2007 runway show in Milan (*above*). McGrath at the Victoria Beckham Spring 2014 show in New York (*right*).

TRADES AT WORK

EARNING POTENTIAL

The US Bureau of Labor Statistics provides estimated wage ranges for most workers in any given job category. The ranges below are from May 2023. While these estimates provide a sense of what you could expect to earn, actual salaries can vary greatly depending on where you work, your amount of experience, and any specialized skills you have.

GROW YOUR POTENTIAL

Whatever salary you start at, there are various ways to grow your earning potential throughout your career. Here are a few ways you can boost your income while continuing to do what you love.

Specialize in a specific type of service. For example, you might decide to be your salon's expert in hair extensions, seek additional training in advanced skin treatments, or focus exclusively on special effects makeup. In time, you may be able to charge more for your expertise.

Become your own boss. When working for an employer, you are typically limited to a set income, no matter how well the business does. But when you're self-employed, your earnings can increase with experience and the success of your business. For some, self-employment means opening a brick-and-mortar shop. Other options that require

JOB CATEGORY	ANNUAL SALARY
Hairdressers, Hairstylists, and Cosmetologists	$29,000–$47,000
Barbers	$30,000–$49,000
Manicurists and Pedicurists	$31,000–$37,000
Skincare Specialists	$33,000–$59,000
Makeup Artists, Theatrical and Performance	$23,000–$101,000

less of a financial investment can include renting out a chair or room at an existing salon. And if your equipment and supplies are portable, you can create a mobile business in which you travel to clients.

Break into a new area of the industry. Say you transition from doing haircuts at a salon to styling hair for commercial photo shoots. Or you're a makeup artist who decides to specialize in eyelash extensions. Or maybe you use your expertise as an esthetician to become a consultant for a skin care brand. If you get creative, you may discover multiple paths that branch from the one you're currently on!

FINANCIAL SMARTS

However you're making money, it's important to manage your finances wisely.

If you have an employer, you will receive a regular paycheck from them. This income will be your wages minus taxes. If your employer offers health insurance, retirement savings, or any other benefits, those will also be deducted from your take-home pay. Financial experts recommend you put about 20 percent of each paycheck into savings and try to keep an emergency fund with enough money to cover three to six months' worth of living expenses.

If you are self-employed, you will receive payments directly from your various clients. You'll need to track this income along with your business expenses, such as rent and supplies. Self-employed individuals must also pay their own taxes, generally four times a year, since they don't have an employer withholding taxes from each paycheck. Business owners use the remaining profits to pay themselves as well as fund savings accounts—for both themselves and the business.

If you have employees, you must pay both yourself and your employees. You must also manage your company's payroll, employee benefits, business insurance, and more. This takes a lot of work and organization. But hiring employees can bring many benefits, such as new skills and increased profits. It can also give you more time to focus on growing the business.

DO WHAT YOU LOVE!

Being a hair, nail, or skin specialist requires stamina, organization, attention to detail, and more. Finding success in this work can take years of training. It also takes a commitment to keep learning and growing your skills. Many beauty professionals find the time and effort is worth the rewards of being creative, building relationships, and boosting clients' confidence.

Maybe your goal is to work at a luxury spa. Maybe you have your sights set on opening your own barbershop. Or perhaps you want a weekend gig doing makeup for weddings. As long as you do what you love, you'll love what you do.

GLOSSARY

accentuate–to emphasize or make more noticeable.

articulate–to clearly and effectively express oneself.

complexion–tone or look of the skin.

dermatology–a medical discipline that deals with the skin.

dexterity–physically competent, skilled, and graceful. Dexterous means to do something with skill or grace.

eczema–a reoccurring skin condition that can make the skin inflamed. Some symptoms include skin redness and itching.

efficient–able to produce a desired result, especially without wasting time or energy. Efficiently means to do a task in a way that does not waste time or energy.

embellishment–a decoration or adornment added to make something more attractive.

entrepreneur–one who organizes, manages, and accepts the risks of a business or an enterprise.

franchise–the right granted to someone to sell goods or services in a particular place. The business operating with this right is also known as a franchise.

inclusive–including everyone.

lead sulfide–an element made up of lead and sulfur.

network–an interconnected group of people or computers.

nonverbal–not speaking aloud or using words.

periodic–repeating at regular periods in time.

pigment–a substance that gives color to something.

potential–capable of being or becoming.

prosthetic–a device or object that was made to change the look of a body part.

refugee–a person who flees to another country for safety and protection.

rosacea–a reoccurring skin disorder where the skin becomes inflamed. Usually this happens on the nose, forehead, and chin.

rotary—turning on a center point.

silicone—a type of rubbery plastic.

specialize—to develop expertise in a certain area, called a specialty. A person who does this is a specialist.

stamina—the power to endure fatigue, disease, or hardship.

synthetic—something that is human-made by a chemical process.

ultrasonic—a frequency unable to be heard by the human ear.

ultraviolet light—a type of light that cannot be seen with the human eye.

ventilation—the movement of air through a room or other space.

ONLINE RESOURCES

To learn more about trades in cosmetology, please visit **abdobooklinks.com** or scan this QR code. These links are routinely monitored and updated to provide the most current information available.

INDEX